"OTAY!"

THE BILLY "BUCKWHEAT" THOMAS STORY

BY WILLIAM THOMAS, JR. AND DAVID W. MENEFEE

"OTAY!"
THE BILLY "BUCKWHEAT" THOMAS STORY
©2010 WILLIAM THOMAS, JR.

ALL RIGHTS RESERVED.

No part of this book may be reproduced in any form or by any means, electronic, mechanical, digital, photocopying, or recording, except for in the inclusion of a review, without permission in writing from the publisher.

Published in the USA by:

BEARMANOR MEDIA
P.O. BOX 71426
ALBANY, GEORGIA 31708
www.BearManorMedia.com

ISBN-10: 1-59393-519-6 (alk. paper)
ISBN-13: 978-1-59393-519-1 (alk. paper)

ALL PHOTOS AND ILLUSTRATIONS FROM THE BILL THOMAS, JR. ESTATE COLLECTION.

CO-WRITTEN AND EDITED BY DAVID W. MENEFEE.

BOOK DESIGN AND LAYOUT BY VALERIE THOMPSON.

Dedication

This book is dedicated to the young at heart,

wherever they are around the world.

Jesus said, "Bring the little ones to me."

The love of children will keep

the circle of life going forever.

"OTAY!"

Acknowledgments

We thank the following people who contributed to this book:

Stephanie Andrade and staff at Verbum Dei Boys School

Richard Bann

Tommy Bond, Jr.

Brian Garcia

Miriam Howard

Richard Lamparski

Dash Morrison

Ben Ohmart

Richard Ottens

Allan Ottens

Cindy Snavely

Miriam Theus

Valerie Thompson

Cynthia Williams, Media Librarian at Foshay Learning Center

Introduction

Childhood lives in the memories of every person as the most wonderful, magical time in their lives. Fantasies and delight color every day in a child's life, and no recollection of those years was ever more affectionate and humorous than those captured in motion pictures by the Hal Roach Studios. With their *Our Gang* comedies, which were later known as *The Little Rascals*, the children never grew up. Their real lives were another story.

This book celebrates William Thomas, the man known as "Buckwheat," one of the most beloved characters in the history of those films. His heritage grew to be more than the ninety-three comedies in which he appeared as Buckwheat. He was a husband, father, soldier, and friend. Several generations have come to know the boy as if he was a real person, but few knew Billy, the man behind the myth.

"OTAY!"

In the first years of the twentieth century, motion pictures became popular as entertainment. In every town, "nickelodeons" sprang up in tiny stores, and new films arrived daily that brought escapism to country yokels who barely knew how to read and to urban immigrants who could barely speak English. Their escape from life's monotony came from watching the movies. For a nickel, they could watch thrilling melodramas and short comedies. They plunked down millions of coins, and the film industry rushed out as much new product as they could manufacture to quench the public thirst for new stories.

The nearly year-round sunshine in California attracted film companies to Hollywood, Los Angeles, and the wild suburbs where orange groves and Eucalyptus plants grew taller than a man's head. In one of these dusty boom towns, a young man named Will Thomas met and married a pretty girl named Mattie.

THE BILLY "BUCKWHEAT" THOMAS STORY

Hollywood in 1905 before filmmakers invaded the quiet city. The street running horizontally down the center is Hollywood Boulevard, and the home with the oriental cupola still exists today, carefully preserved by the American Society of Cinematographers. Into that valley or orange groves, the grandparents of Billy Thomas arrived.

"OTAY!"

Hal Roach (1892–1992), a mule skinner, wrangler, and gold prospector turned truck driver, journeyed to Hollywood looking for an easy way to earn $5 a day. Roach first picked up a job posing in a gambling scene in which nobody knew that the roulette wheel and the ball should go in opposite directions. He set the men straight and was on his way.

Roach worked as an extra one day, or an assistant the next day. He saw men become directors based on their willingness to be enthusiastic and imaginative when the first rays of the morning sun were just poking through the treetops. In 1913, he met comedian Harold Lloyd. With financing from a small inheritance, Roach began writing, directing, and producing a series of short film comedies starring the actor. Encouraged by success, Roach attracted other stars, and he began producing comedy films with animals and children.

THE BILLY "BUCKWHEAT" THOMAS STORY

Producer Hal Roach and versatile comedian Harold Lloyd were making films together in the early silent era.

"OTAY!"

One day in 1921, Hal Roach looked through the window of his office and watched some kids playing in a nearby lot. They were arguing over a stick as if was the most important thing in the world. Their antics fascinated him and gave birth to the idea for the *Our Gang* comedy series.

The series was originally called *Hal Roach's Rascals*, and the title of the first film in the series was *Our Gang*. Children were painstakingly cast to represent a cross section of every neighborhood gang, including a leader and his sidekick, a tag-along toddler, a bully, a pretty girl, and a dog. Children included both African-Americans and females during an era when discrimination against both groups was commonplace. The gang often engaged with snobbish rich kids, bossy adults, and demanding parents. Roach hit gold with the winning formula, and the *Our Gang* series found immediate success with audiences.

THE BILLY "BUCKWHEAT" THOMAS STORY

Back in the silent movie era, the kids from the gang were not much different from the later kids. As each child outgrew their roles, replacements were found.

"OTAY!"

On March 16, 1926, Hal Roach changed distributors for his comedies from Pathé to MGM. For three years, he delivered silent comedies starring Laurel and Hardy, Charley Chase, *Our Gang*, and the Roach All-Stars, among others. Then in early March 1929, sound pictures brought their voices to the screen. Teaching scripted dialogue to children as young as three years old required painstaking repetition. They chose to keep dialogue to a minimum and emphasize action and sight gags. The new formula blended superbly.

In April after the Roach sound stages were converted for sound recording, they produced *Small Talk*, their first all-talking picture. After another year passed, the gang lost Joe, Jean, and Harry, and they added Norman "Chubby" Chaney, Dorothy DeBorba, Matthew "Stymie" Beard, Donald Haines, and Jackie Cooper. Since the series' success continued, they then knew they could bring in any new child without missing a beat.

THE BILLY "BUCKWHEAT" THOMAS STORY

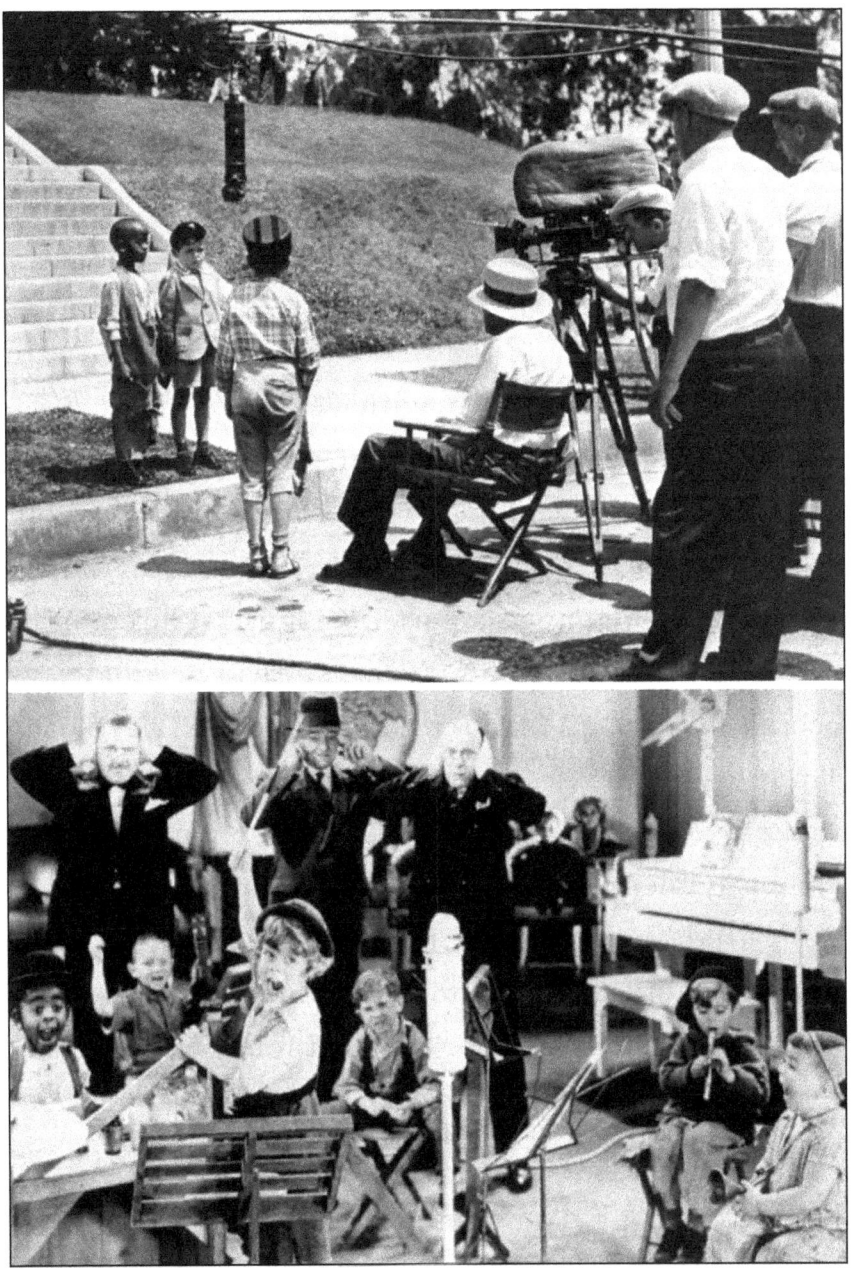

Microphones were always nearby in those early talking pictures. (TOP) Director Bob McGowan, Stymie, and Dickie filming an early talking comedy, *Free Wheeling* (1932). (BOTTOM) While making *Mike Fright* (1934), the kids posed for this publicity picture.

"OTAY!"

In 1930, lighthearted background music scores were first added to enliven scenes that were primarily visual, and the first use of a soundtrack in an *Our Gang* film came with *When the Wind Blows* (1930). Orchestral versions of popular tunes were initially used to accompany the children's antics, but when NBC's general music director Leroy Shield joined the company as a part-time musical director, he and Marvin Hatley devised inspired, original jazz scores. *Pups is Pups* (1930) first featured the "Hal Roach Happy-Go-Lucky Trio" performing a delightfully breezy, remarkable score with a saxophone solo that smoothly blended the often choppy film editing. They delighted in watching the kids work, and they composed music that matched the unusual things they observed them doing. For the next four years, the trio expanded to a sixty-five-piece orchestra, and Shield and Hatley's scores brought sprightly themes that synchronized along with the gang's on-screen shenanigans.

THE BILLY "BUCKWHEAT" THOMAS STORY

Spanky McFarland joined the *Our Gang* series, and with more cast changes in the wind, Billy's opportunity was soon to come.

"OTAY!"

In February 1931, three-year-old George "Spanky" McFarland joined the gang in *Free Eats*. At first, he appeared as the group's tag-along toddler, but his angelic face was so cute, hardly a week passed before producers crafted *Spanky*, a comedy centered on the toddler.

On March 12, 1931, William "Buckwheat" Thomas was born in Los Angeles, California, the only child of Mattie Elizabeth and Will Thomas, a janitor at the Wilton Apartments in Hollywood.

In 1932, Dickie Moore, veteran of at least twenty-eight films, joined the gang along with Dickie Jackson, John "Uh-huh" Collum, and Tommy Bond. The following year, Moore moved on to appear in more feature films and Wheezer and Dorothy left the series. There were rumblings going on about Matthew Beard. He was outgrowing his role as "Stymie," and producers started thinking about replacing him. The stage was set for the arrival of Billy Thomas.

THE BILLY "BUCKWHEAT" THOMAS STORY

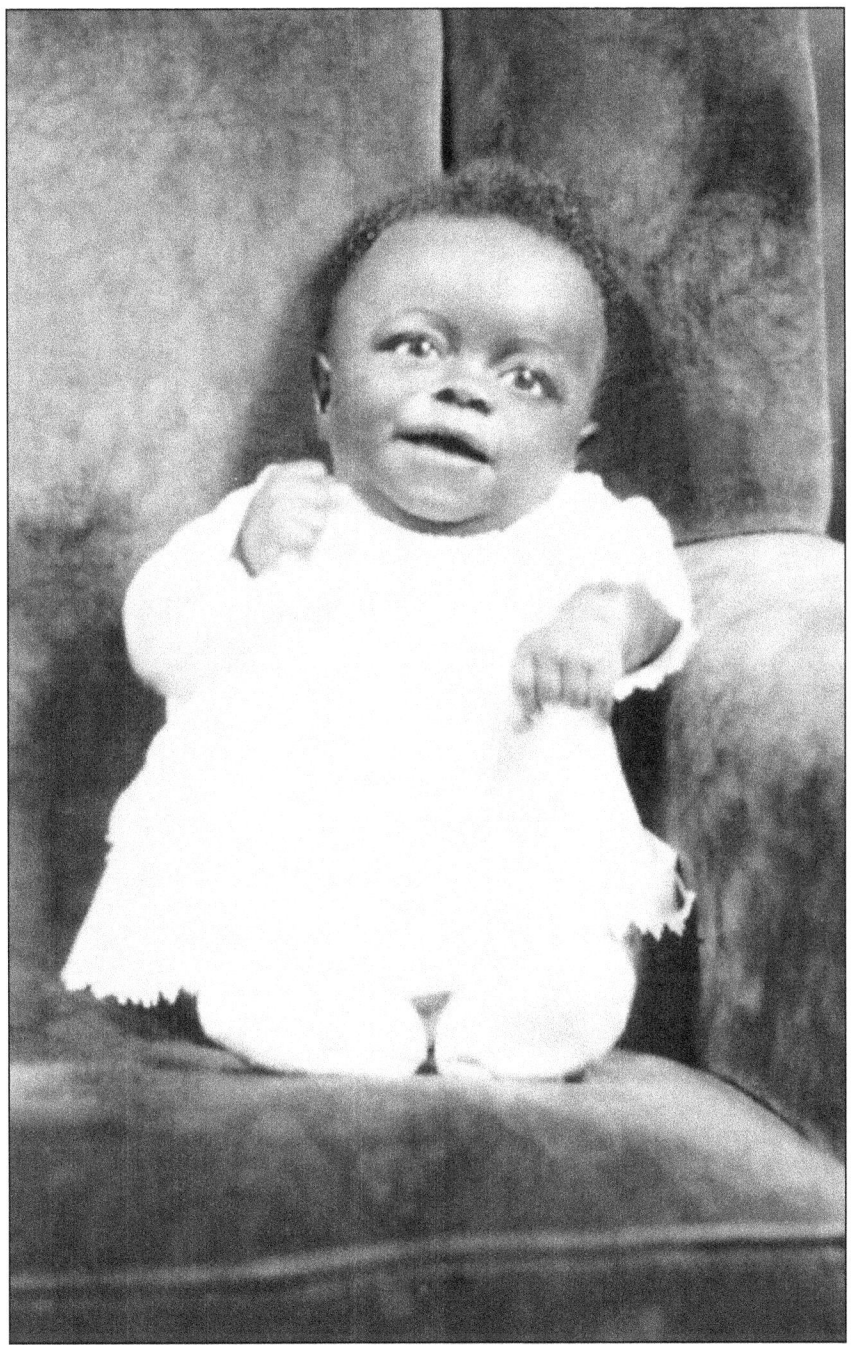

Baby Billy Thomas at home on his mother's crushed-velvet sofa.

"OTAY!"

In late 1933, *Our Gang* veteran director Robert McGowan wearied from the strain and left the series along with Dickie, Wheezer, and Dorothy. Their departures left a void, and the series went on a four-month holiday, while theatergoers saw Spanky and his parents, played by Gay Seabrooke and Emerson Treacy, as the main characters in McGowan's last two *Our Gang* comedies, *Bedtime Worries* and *Wild Poses*. Upheaval was in the air.

Hal Roach cast about for replacements. The kids came back from vacation, and veteran comedy director Gus Meins, who had directed some films with Charlie Chase and Laurel and Hardy, took charge and successfully shepherded the whole gang through the stylish and witty *Hi' Neighbor!*, and then he turned to the task of seeing what could be done about replacing Matthew Beard. Billy and his parents were waiting in the wings, unaware of the backstage drama taking place behind *Our Gang* productions.

THE BILLY "BUCKWHEAT" THOMAS STORY

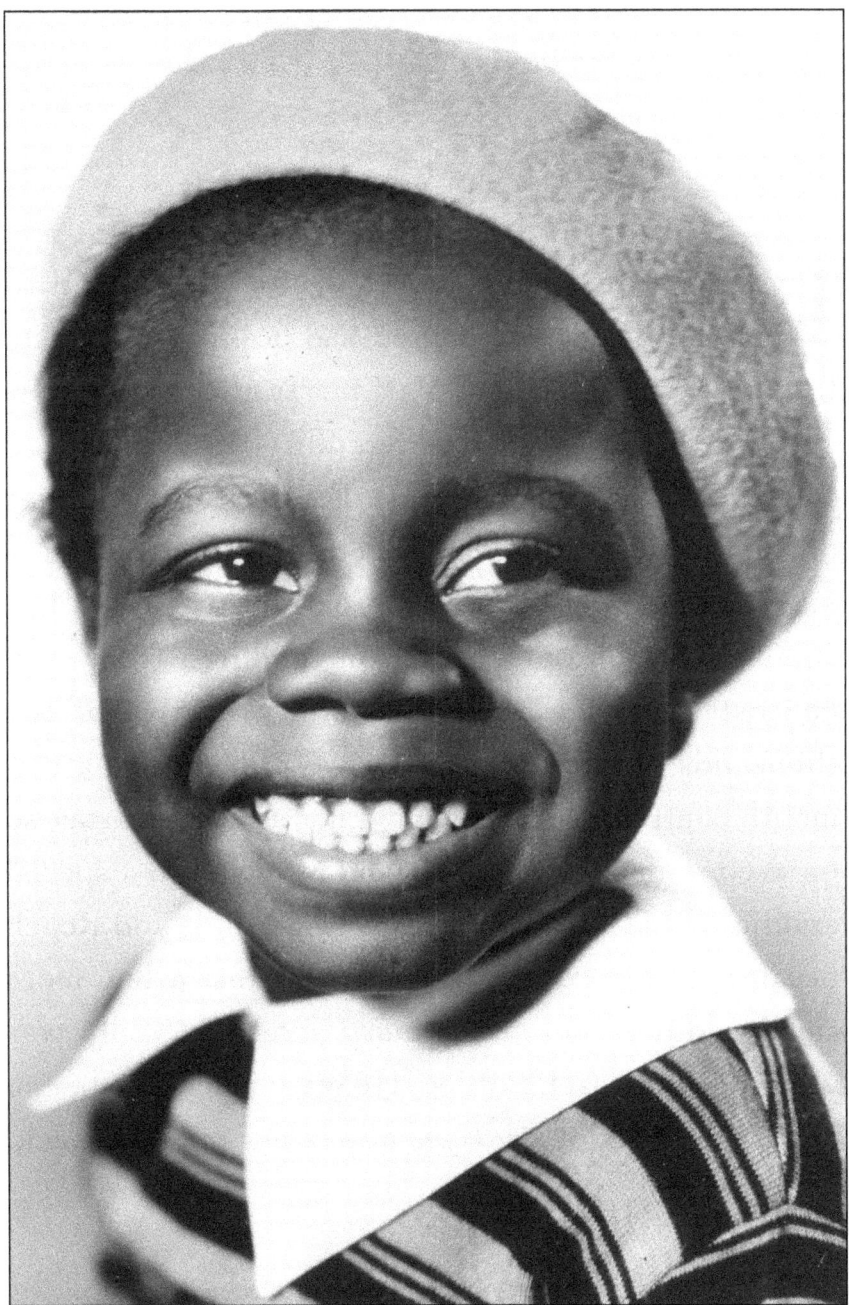

Billy was waiting in the wings as a replacement for Matthew "Stymie" Beard, who had outgrown his role in the *Our Gang* series.

"OTAY!"

In 1934, Hal Roach searched for a black kid to replace Stymie, who himself had been a replacement for the early character, Farina. To discover a new child with the magical personality needed, Roach staged monthly talent contests. Each Saturday, hoards of kids prodded by determined mothers descended on the Lincoln Theatre on Central Avenue in Los Angeles. Roach only chose four children from each contest to do a screen test, and only two of the thousands of auditioning kids were to receive a six-month contract. Mattie wanted her son to be a star, so on Wednesday, October 10, she took him to a special audition. One look at Billy's eyes and smile and Roach became enamored of the boy. After just a few more small auditions for preliminary screeners, Billy was ushered into Roach's office. He was engaged to be the newest member of *Our Gang* at a salary of $40 a week.

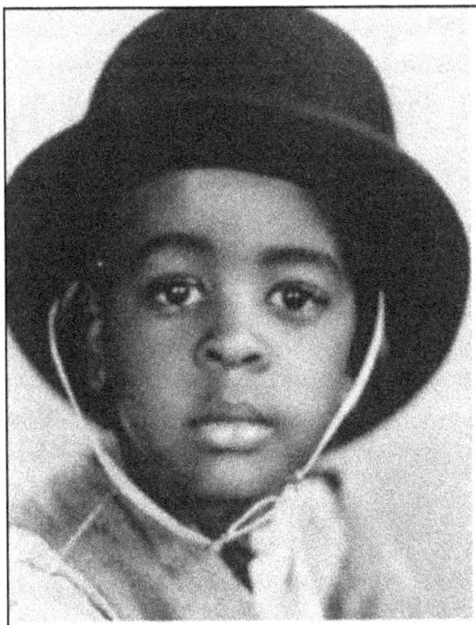

THE BILLY "BUCKWHEAT" THOMAS STORY

(TOP) "Stymie" Beard had outgrown his role in *Our Gang*, and when Hal Roach's staff finally selected Billy as his replacement, (BOTTOM) Loew's Incorporated had to petition the Superior Court of the State of California for approval to put the minor to work.

"OTAY!"

When Mattie successfully won a contract for Billy's appearances in motion pictures, she scored a victory that few "stage mothers" achieve, and to do so with an African-American child was more than a win; her achievement was a triumph for all Black women and men who were struggling to succeed in the business world that was evolving one day at a time, one minor victory at a notch. Years would pass before Hattie McDaniel would win an Academy Award for her work. In the meantime, Mattie set about transforming Billy into a new star.

In real life, Billy was just a normal, happy boy, who was content with the toys that brought joy into his life. Under the glare of lights in a photographer's studio, Mattie carefully crafted his new image in a comic style that was not unlike a pint-sized Charlie Chaplin, complete with a cap and cane.

THE BILLY "BUCKWHEAT" THOMAS STORY

Billy in real life (LEFT) and Billy as his grandmother restyled him for films, a pint-sized Charlie Chaplin complete with hat and cane.

"OTAY!"

The Hal Roach Studios were located at 8822 Washington Boulevard at the corner of Washington and National in Culver City. Most of the *Our Gang* comedies were made there, and actors and crew affectionately called the studio "The Lot of Fun." In 1933, there no freeways, so getting there was no easy journey for sleepy child actors and their determined mothers.

"My mother used to drive me back and forth to the studio," Billy remembered. "It was a long drive down Washington back then because there was no freeway. I had to get up pretty early in the morning. I had all kinds of toys. Every new toy that came along, I wanted and I had. My father bought me anything I wanted. I took my toys with me in the car, and I sometimes ate ice cream along the way. My mother made sure we were always on time."

THE BILLY "BUCKWHEAT" THOMAS STORY

Mattie Elizabeth Thomas, Billy's mother, who was the driving force behind Billy's career as a child star.

"OTAY!"

Hal Roach's production team began setting up Billy for success. Various names were thrown out for consideration, but the name that appealed most to them was one that followed the formula long established with Farina and Stymie, the two kids that had been enormously popular and firmly entrenched as key ingredients to the chemistry of the old gang.

Since the "Farina" name had sprung from a breakfast food made from middlings produced in flour milling, the ever-popular Aunt Jemima Buckwheat Pancake Mix proved equally inspirational. "Buckwheat" captured the home-spun essence of an *Our Gang* child. The name had been occasionally used off and on for eleven years during the series, but suddenly, plans were made to crown Billy as the next "Buckwheat."

"I enjoyed it," Billy said. "We had a lot of fun together. Just like a family. We went to school together, played together, and laughed together. It was great!"

THE BILLY "BUCKWHEAT" THOMAS STORY

Aunt Jemima Buckwheat Pancake Mix ad as it appeared in magazines around America the year of Billy's birth. The tasty breakfast treat served as the inspiration for his character's name.

"OTAY!"

Billy did not become "Buckwheat" right away. *For Pete's Sake* (1934), the film in which he first appeared, featured the boy as just another member of the gang. Carlena Beard, kid sister of Matthew "Stymie" Beard, played "Buckwheat." For the next three films, Willie Mae Taylor played the female "Buckwheat" character.

Billy started out as what seemed to be another little girl, although no one knew for sure what sex he was supposed to be, adding a certain mystique to the character. He wore a dress or sometimes diapers and was good at crying on cue. Robert Blake recalled that Billy hated wearing those costumes and tore them off when shooting was finished.

In *Washee Ironee* (1934), Billy's third appearance earned a noticeable spot. While the gang played football outside, he sat in the bleachers gauging the action through binoculars made with a pair of soda pop bottles bound together.

THE BILLY "BUCKWHEAT" THOMAS STORY

Billy did not become "Buckwheat" right away. In several of his first appearances, producers dressed him in androgynous clothing or as a little girl. He hated wearing girl's clothes, and tore them off as soon as his work was over.

"OTAY!"

For some weeks, Billy was gradually groomed to replace "Stymie."

"I couldn't understand when I saw they were bringing William along, even though I went through the same thing in replacing Farina," remembered Matthew Beard years later on a television talk show. "But they brought William out when I was beginning to get too large, and I just had that funny feeling; I heard the footsteps, but I didn't want to go."

Jackie Lynn Taylor and Marriane Edwards, semi-regular kids in the gang, joined the series along with Leonard Kibrick as the neighborhood bully. Kids came and went, but Spanky and his mugging held the stories together, and Gus Mein's ingenious camerawork kept the pacing smooth.

In *Anniversary Trouble* (1935), Billy played the daughter of a household maid, Mandy, played by the delightful Hattie McDaniel. The toddler endearingly perplexes audiences with his garbled speech, and in one scene, Spanky disguises as "Buckwheat."

THE BILLY "BUCKWHEAT" THOMAS STORY

When working on films, the *Our Gang* kids had plenty of time for fun and games. Billy watched Darla attempting to play golf, but sadly, she played like a little girl.

"OTAY!"

Billy was all boy, so they gave him the "Buckwheat" name, and in his next film role, the legend finally took form. Over the course of the next year, he appeared in a half-dozen of the comedies, often dressed androgynously. Billy became firmly entrenched as one of the gang

Teacher's Beau (1935) featured the final appearance of Matthew "Stymie" Beard. By the age of ten, he had outgrown the gang and was completely in the background. Cameras shifted to Billy, who jumped into the goings-on with great enthusiasm.

In the *Our Gang Follies of 1936*, the entire gang took center stage in a song and dance musical review. Not a single adult appeared in the story about the kids producing a show in their cellar theater. The innovative musical even won favorable reviews *The New York Evening Journal, The Film Daily, Daily Variety*, and *Motion Picture Daily*.

THE BILLY "BUCKWHEAT" THOMAS STORY

In the early months of 1935, Matthew "Stymie" Beard had departed the series, and Billy took over as the new kid in the gang. His wide-open face and expressive eyes that captured Hal Roach's attention immediately caught notice from audiences.

"OTAY!"

The Our Gang Café served up breakfast, lunch, or dinner every day of the week except Sunday, treating both studio personnel as well as the public to informal dining with actors who dropped in while wearing funny-looking costumes. Patrons saw Buckwheat and the other *Our Gang* kids, Oliver Hardy, Charlie Chaplin, William S. Hart, and even Greta Garbo snacking on meals along side tourists and townspeople.

A casual atmosphere held everyone's ego at bay, while hot meals were served up to keep the studio personnel going at full pace, as well as to entertain tourists and passers-by. The interior was decorated with oil paintings by Jean Negulesco, who was then working as a studio writer, but later achieved distinction as a film director.

A full plate lunch, dessert, and coffee cost a patron 35¢. Dinner and wine cost a mere 65¢, and the costliest entree on the menu was steak smothered with mushrooms at $1.65 for two. At the Our Gang Café, having buckwheat for breakfast took on a whole new meaning.

THE BILLY "BUCKWHEAT" THOMAS STORY

(TOP) Alfalfa, Harold, Darla, Spanky, and Buckwheat inside the Our Gang Café. (BOTTOM) Billy and Mattie outside the Our Gang Café.

"OTAY!"

Children in the *Our Gang* series were replaced when they outgrew their roles and others were brought in because of their unique personalities. Darla Hood and Eugene "Porky" Lee, joined the gang, as Buckwheat gradually evolved into a male character.

By 1934, many theater owners were booking double feature programs and dropping two-reel comedies from their bills. Hal Roach also experimented with an *Our Gang* feature film. *General Spanky* starred Spanky, Buckwheat, and Alfalfa in a Civil War comedy/romance, but it was a box office disappointment. Roach debated discontinuing *Our Gang*, but Louis B. Mayer, MGM production head and the series' distributor, convinced him to continue with a new string of twelve shorter one-reel comedies. Former assistant director Gordon Douglas directed *Bored of Education* (1936), their first one-reel *Our Gang* short, and the film won an Academy Award for Best Short Subject. Once again, the series was on track for success.

THE BILLY "BUCKWHEAT" THOMAS STORY

The *Our Gang* kids loved all their various directors. Each man had a special rapport with child actors, and managed to direct them through their scenes despite the watchful, eagle eyes of all their mothers, who were always lingering nearby on the sets.

"OTAY!"

In real life, Billy and most of the *Our Gang* children were also bored of education. Early cast member Jackie Cooper recalled in his autobiography, ". . . working was good because when I worked, I didn't have to go to school . . . the longer I stayed on the set, the less time I had to spend in school—a simple equation that even I could understand. We worked from eight in the morning until six at night like everybody else."

Compulsory education laws mandated that the education of child actor not be disrupted while the child is working. Whether Billy was enrolled in public school, private school, or home school, he did his schoolwork under the supervision of a teacher while on the set. Billy drifted in and out of grammar school, supposedly attending the Grant School that was not far from the Gower-Sunset intersection.

THE BILLY "BUCKWHEAT" THOMAS STORY

Billy was no different than any other boy. When he was off the set, he enjoyed fishing and playing with toys.

"OTAY!"

In 1939, the California Child Actor's Bill, also known as the Coogan Act or Coogan Bill, was passed by the State of California in response to the plight of child actor Jackie Coogan. He earned millions of dollars as a beloved child actor only to learn upon reaching adulthood that his unscrupulous parents had squandered almost all of his money. To safeguard future child actors like Billy from such atrocities, the law safeguarded a portion of their earnings, but Loew's Incorporated did not deduct the requirement amount; they left the matter entirely up to his parents.

With each weekly pay check, Billy received a letter from the studio reminding his parents that they were required by law to deduct 10% of his gross salary for the purchase of a United States Savings Bond that was to be recorded in Billy's name. Billy was to receive the accumlated money when he reached the age of twenty-one.

THE BILLY "BUCKWHEAT" THOMAS STORY

March 23, 1943

Master William Thomas, Jr.,
c/o Metro-Goldwyn-Mayer Studios,
Culver City, California.

Dear Master Thomas:

   We hand you herewith your weekly pay check with the customary deductions.

   Your attention is called to the provisions of the court's order to the effect that 10% of your gross weekly salary must be used by you for the purchase of United States Savings Bonds. We are not making this deduction from your check. Accordingly, you must see to it that that part of the court's order is carried out, since your failure to purchase bonds according to the order, would be construed by the court as a violation of the order.

        Yours very truly,

        LOEW'S INCORPORATED

        BY [signature]

ea

In 1943, MGM and Loew's, Inc. sent a letter to "Master William Thomas, Jr. along with his weekly pay check. They made special note of "the court's order to the effect that 10% of your gross weekly salary must be used by you for the purchase of United States Savings Bonds."

"OTAY!"

In 1936, Adolph Hitler tried to use the summer Olympics in Berlin to glorify his Nazi dictatorship and bring his Aryan vision onto a world stage, but his plan failed when Black American sprinter Jesse Owens magnificently won the first of his four gold medals. Newsreels of the momentous event were shown around the world at the same time that little Billy was seen by millions of people nearly each week at the movies. *Two Too Young* (1936) brought his Buckwheat character clearly into focus and made full use of his camaraderie with Eugene "Porky" Lee. Writers required them to closely follow a sixteen-page shooting script. The plot carefully wove around their personalities and poked fun at their incoherent speech. The comic tag-along team of Buckwheat and Porky, along with the well-known interactions between Alfalfa and Spanky, became as familiar to audiences as the loveable Laurel and Hardy team.

THE BILLY "BUCKWHEAT" THOMAS STORY

Porky and Buckwheat telling each other about the secret hiding place during the "war" in the full-length film, *General Spanky*. Both boys had a strong rapport with each other, and they were often featured in antics together.

"OTAY!"

They were small in size, yet larger than life. No Hollywood stars could have attracted bigger crowds that the *Our Gang* members when they made live, personal appearances. For most of the 1936 summer, the *Our Gang* kids toured the country and met their fans. When the kids trooped to the Duluth movie theater, Spanky, Darla, "Alfalfa" and "Buckwheat" accompanied Joe Cobb, who served as Master of Ceremonies. They came early and stayed late, sharing popcorn with the populace and candy with the kids. They sat through so many shows that the management could clear the theater only by luring the crowds to the stage door with a promise of autographs. Kids and adults thrilled to meet the child comics in person. When famed columnist Louella O. Parsons reported on the phenomena in her syndicated newspaper column, she wrote, "Even Greta Garbo herself couldn't have brought a bigger crowd."

THE BILLY "BUCKWHEAT" THOMAS STORY

The *Our Gang* kids went on many promotional tours. So he would stand out, Billy's mother helped him practice some funny bits of business and amusing things to say, which amazed the other kids when he surprised them all with his wit.

"OTAY!"

The Hal Roach Studio was charmed by the reception afforded Billy. None of the Black American boys and girls in the *Our Gang* series had struck such a responsive chord with audiences. With the release of *General Spanky*, Billy was singled out for commendation, even though Spanky's name was in the film title. The following article appeared in newspapers around the world in February 1937, and is quoted here from the *La Crosse Tribune and Leader-Press*:

"The greatest colored boy comedian ever to appear on the screen is the claim made by Producer Hal Roach for "Buckwheat" Thomas, the little-four-year-old member of *Our Gang*, who has an outstanding part in the feature length comedy, *General Spanky*, showing at the Wisconsin theater for the last times today. Buckwheat is teamed with Spanky McFarland in this epic of a youngster's loyalty and bravery during the great conflict between the North and South."

THE BILLY "BUCKWHEAT" THOMAS STORY

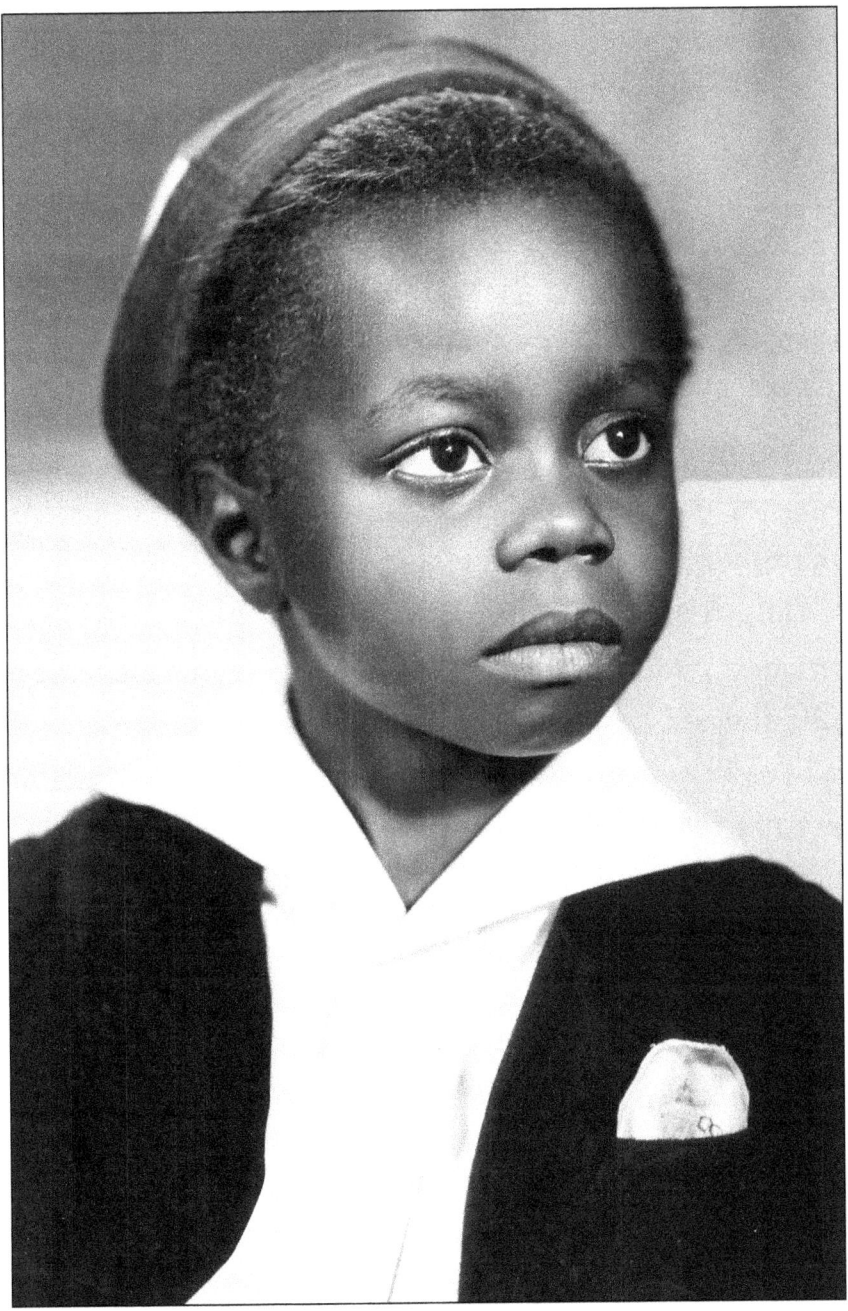

Posing for portraits was no fun for kids, but Billy stood and sat in front of photographer's cameras and lights like a professional.

"OTAY!"

Kids of all ages still love to imitate Buckwheat. One of his most common expressions was what veterans called a "double-take" with a look of shock or surprise. In many of the *Our Gang* comedies, his alarm was often accented by his hat flying up off his head, his natural hair suddenly standing on end, or his pigtails flaring out like waving arms.

Billy remembered those moments. "I originally had braided pigtails in the series . . . but only in the series. Off the set, I wore my hair natural. In those scenes where I was supposed to be scared and the pigtails or my hat flew up in what looked like horror, they were actually connected to wires that were pulled off camera so it would look like they were shooting up like that. They used great big fans, too, to blow my hair or hat up suddenly."

THE BILLY "BUCKWHEAT" THOMAS STORY

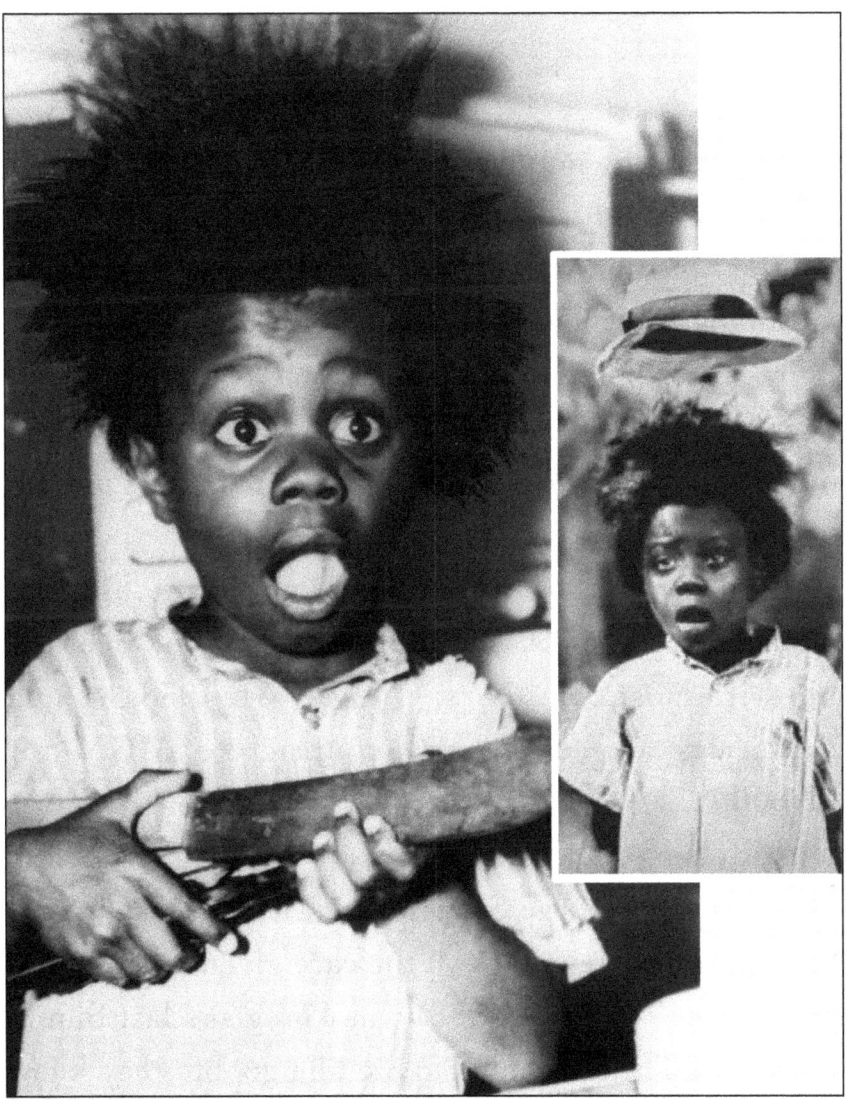

"In those scenes where I was supposed to be scared and the pigtails or my hat flew up in what looked like horror, they were actually connected to wires that were pulled off camera," Billy said.

"OTAY!"

With the move to one-reel shorts and after gradual cast changes, Buckwheat, Spanky, Alfalfa, Darla, and Porky rounded out the troupe most fans remember best. Tommy Bond as "Butch," the bully, his crony, Sidney "The Woim" Kibrick, and the bookworm, Darwood "Waldo" Kaye, wandered in and out of the *Our Gang* neighborhood, often in his pursuit of Darla's affections.

Throughout 1937, Hal Roach kept a watchful eye on declining profits, as double features took over the bill with most exhibitors. On May 31, 1938, he sold the series and everyone's contract to MGM for $25,000.

Producer Jack Chertok and directors Gordon Douglas and George Sidney kept the series rolling off their assembly line with all the care given to a feature, but *Aladdin's Lantern* (1938) was Douglas's last film in the series. The kids hated to see him go, but they knew they were actors and continued working as they were told.

THE BILLY "BUCKWHEAT" THOMAS STORY

In 1938, the *Our Gang* kids moved to the prestigious MGM studios, where many of the greatest movie stars worked. Clark Gable was Billy's favorite.

"OTAY!"

In 1939, Billy was eight years old. He continued in the *Our Gang* series even though cast changes were again taking place. Porky was replaced by Mickey Gubitosi, who was later known as Robert Blake. The MGM-produced shorts were often filled with creative sight gags. In *Alfalfa's Aunt* (1939), Buckwheat's hair stands on end at the sound of screaming, and when Porky sniffs smelling salts, his hat flies into the air. However, MGM insisted on keeping some of the kids in the series until they were in their early teens, and Alfalfa's increasingly unfunny, squeaky singing began to wear thin. The kids' performances were stilted and they were not good enough actors to perform fully scripted dialogue. They recited the words stiffly instead of speaking naturally. Adult characters and moral lessons took the place of spontaneous actions, and the films were not as well-received by audiences as in earlier years.

THE BILLY "BUCKWHEAT" THOMAS STORY

Merchandising was big business with films, then and now. When the Our Gang Paint Set was produced, the studio put Spanky and Billy to work showing kids how to have fun painting and coloring with the product. They sold thousands of painting sets.

"OTAY!"

Theaters sandwiched newsreels between *Our Gang* films, and audiences watched with growing alarm as Nazi Germany attacked Britain. On November 8, 1939, Adolf Hitler spoke at a beer hall, unaware that Johann Georg Elser had planted a bomb beneath the speaking platform. He set the timer to go off near the end of Hitler's speech, but the Führer ended earlier than expected. The mistimed explosion failed and the tyrant survived assassination. Franklin Delano Roosevelt found it increasingly difficult to keep America neutral, and audiences found the *Our Gang* shorts increasingly difficult to endure. MGM tried to infuse new life into the series by sweeping out Butch, Waldo, and Alfalfa and bringing in Billy "Froggy" Laughlin and Janet Burston. MGM writers veered the series from the original concept into moral lessons that were educational but unfunny. Only Buckwheat, Darla, and Spanky remained to carry on. They were not getting many laughs.

THE BILLY "BUCKWHEAT" THOMAS STORY

Musicals were big with *Our Gang* fans, and Billy (TOP) greatly enjoyed doing his best impersonation of Cab Calloway. (BOTTOM) The studio never missed an opportunity to use the kids for promotional purposes. A simple picture of them commemorating the New Year in 1936 created a postcard that sold thousands of copies.

"OTAY!"

*O*ur *Gang* directors tried to wring laughs from Buckwheat any way they could. In *The Big Premiere* (1940), he got stuck in a vat of cement; in *Ye Olde Minstrels* (1941), he was a tap-dancing chorus boy, but America had finally entered the war and audiences were scarcely concerned about the antics of overgrown child actors. When the Nazi's sank the *Bizmarck* and then murdered 33,771 Jews at Kiev, filmgoers were much more concerned about Hitler's serious threat to take over the world. On December 7, 1941, the Japanese bombed Pearl Harbor, and interest in the *Our Gang* series waned. In *Helping Hands* (1941), humor disappeared so the gang could show children how to contribute to the national defense program. By the end of 1941, Darla departed from the series and only Buckwheat and Spanky stayed behind, while American men followed the call to arms and enlisted by the thousands.

THE BILLY "BUCKWHEAT" THOMAS STORY

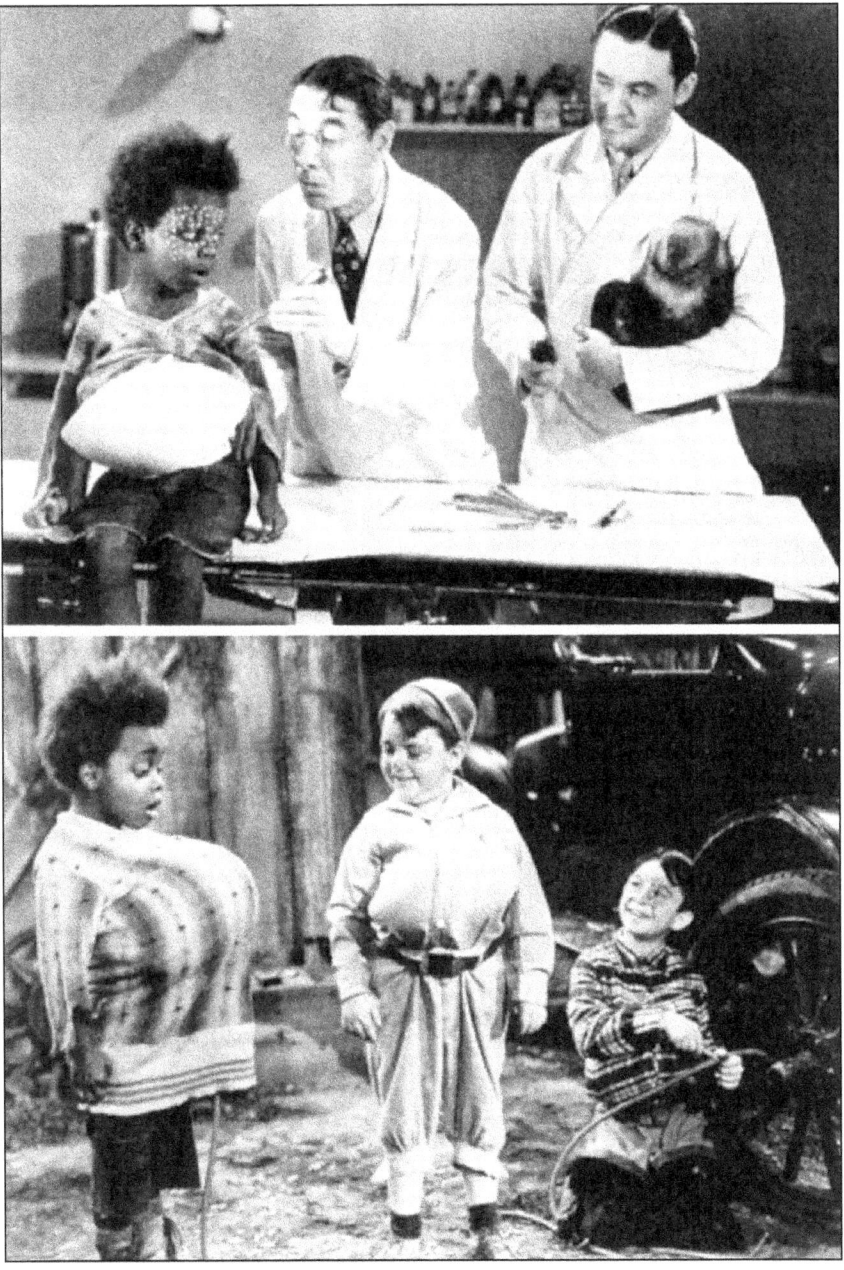

In *Three Smart Boys* (1937), monkeyshines and white measles made for laughs, when Billy as Buckwheat and pals, Spanky and Alfalfa, fake an epidemic in an attempt to close their school.

"OTAY!"

While World War Two was at its height, MGM used the *Our Gang* series as a training ground for up-and-coming stars. In *Melodies Old and New* (1942), Dwayne Hickman, future star of the *Dobie Gillis* television series made an appearance. In *Mighty Lak a Goat* (1942), Ava Gardner played a movie cashier. For the next two years, the series continued with a variety of directors, but MGM lost control of the original concept and all the kids outgrew their roles. By 1944, the *Our Gang* series came to an end with the final comedy, *Tale of a Dog*.

Billy was sad to leave the series and the studio school where the kids went to classes. He was a thirteen-year-old teenager, and his transition to the normal world of regular kids from different backgrounds came as a difficult challenge. They knew he was Buckwheat, and they often made fun of him.

THE BILLY "BUCKWHEAT" THOMAS STORY

Birthday parties were big events in the *Our Gang* kid's real lives, too. (TOP) Darla, Mickey, and Froggy at Billy's birthday party at the MGM Studios. Mattie was always watching nearby, and she is in the left corner. (BOTTOM) Darla's birthday party took place at the same studio.

"OTAY!"

In 1949, Billy married Allie Mae Matthews in Tucson, Arizona. About a year later, Billy's son, William Varde Thomas, Jr. was born on September 15, 1950 at 11:56 p.m. in the Los Angeles County General Hospital. Nineteen-year-old Billy and his seventeen-year-old bride, Allie, lived in an apartment adjacent to Mattie's home on Gramercy Place so that she could oversee every detail of his life.

Billy and Allie enjoyed going out to Central Avenue and the Dunbar Hotel in south central Los Angeles, just down the street from the Lincoln Theater, where Billy had won his first audition. Black athletes, politicians, and entertainers enjoyed the popular playground. Some Black entertainers such as Nat King Cole sculpted their hair with a conditioner to relax the natural texture, and Billy liked to wear his hair in that fashion. He wore Eisenberg and Brooks Brothers suits, and he always dressed up, even on excursions to Disneyland.

THE BILLY "BUCKWHEAT" THOMAS STORY

Billy holding his newborn son, Bill, Jr. Whenever Billy left the house, he always dressed sharply. In the 1950s, his combination of clothes, processed hair, and happy disposition prepared him for meeting fans, who expected an autograph. Billy was happy to sign autographs and pose for pictures.

"OTAY!"

Billy and Allie lived under two shadows: the ghost of "Buckwheat," who trailed Billy throughout his adult life, and the ever-present specter of Mattie. Strong-willed, well-intentioned, and always in charge of Billy, Mattie held tight to the bond with her son. She approved of the marriage, but as the months passed, she resented Allie's influence. She held fast to her management of every day of his life, even requiring him to call from wherever he was and let her know his estimated return time. She extended her control to Allie, going so far as to direct her on small tasks such as picking Billy up from work.

When Bill was around eight years old, he learned of his parent's divorce. He saw no fights nor heard any arguments. His mother simply moved away to a rental apartment not far from Mattie's house. "I don't like your grandmother," was her only explanation.

THE BILLY "BUCKWHEAT" THOMAS STORY

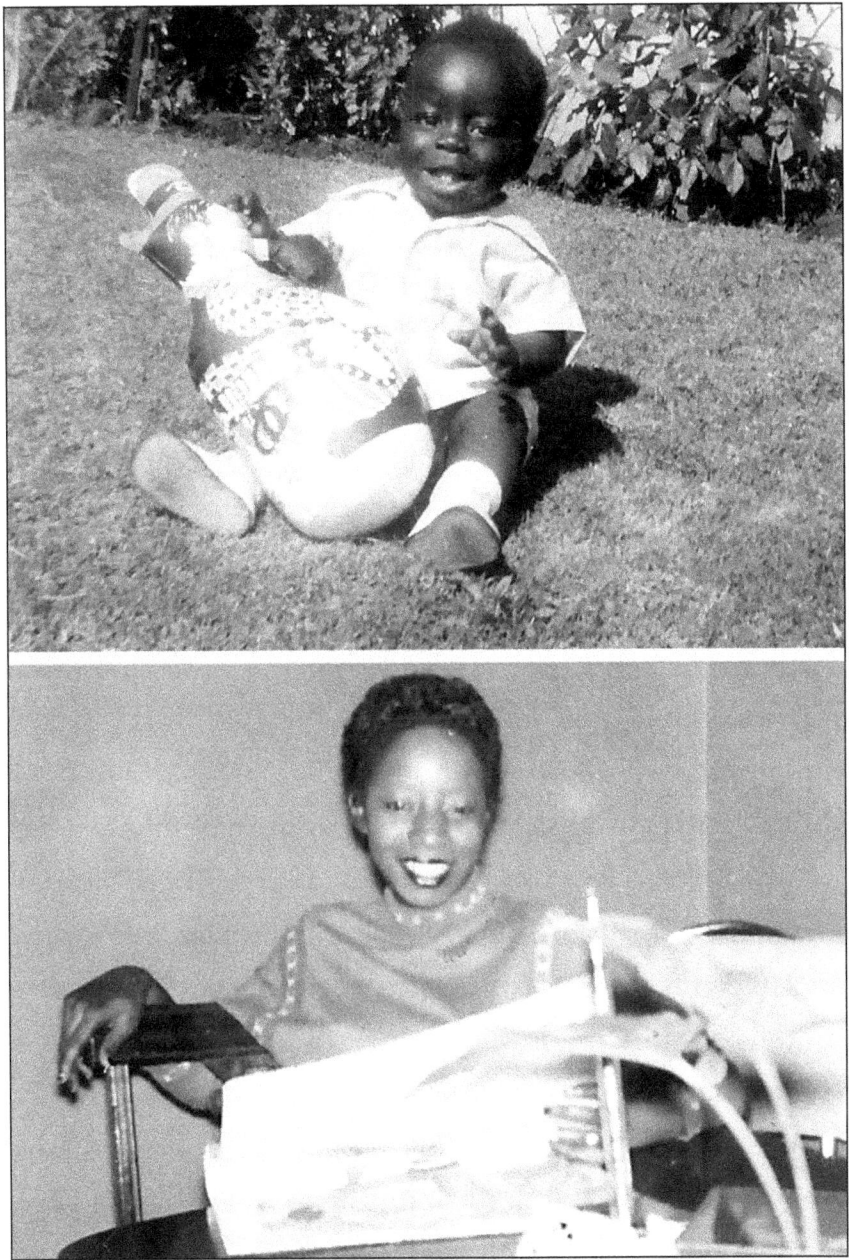

(TOP) One-year-old Bill, Jr. was happy. Billy took him to amusement parks every weekend. (BOTTOM) Bill's mother, Allie Mae, had been an opening dancer for Sammy Davis, Jr. She had difficulty enduring Mattie's overriding influence on their lives.

"OTAY!"

In early 1950, North Korea and South Korea agressively attempted national-peninsula reunification, but escalating skirmishes at the 38th Parallel brought negotiations to a halt.

On Saturday, June 24, 1950, US Secretary of State Dean Acheson telephoned President Harry S. Truman. "Mr. President, I have very serious news," he informed him. "The North Koreans have invaded South Korea." Truman and Acheson agreed that the United States was obligated to repel military aggression and contain the global spread of communism.

On Sunday, June 25, 1950, North Korea fully invaded South Korea. The United States and the United Nations intervened for the South. The call to arms went out, and over the next few years, American men responded by tens of thousands.

On May 14, 1954, Billy was working as a spray painter for the Roll-A-Way Trailer Company in Los Angeles. He left job and home behind and enlisted in the US Army.

THE BILLY "BUCKWHEAT" THOMAS STORY

Billy joined the US Army when the call to arms went out for American men to assist in the Korean conflict. He served proudly.

"OTAY!"

In 1951, the *Our Gang* series was sold to television for $200,000, not enough to completely repay the studio's outstanding debt, but enough to avert ruin. Roach packaged eighty sound *Our Gang* shorts as *The Little Rascals*. Monogram Pictures and its successor, Allied Artists, reissued the films to theaters. In 1955, Interstate Television syndicated the films to television stations. *The Little Rascals* television revival became a phenomenal, modern success story.

The old shorts were not only shown on countless televisions stations across the country, but they were also distributed through various home-movie companies in 8mm and 16mm copies. Dell launched a new series of comic books, and other merchandising gimics brought the old series into the public spotlight more powerfully than when they were originally shown in theaters.

Buckwheat was back again, and an entirely new generation of baby boomer kids enjoyed the *Our Gang* escapades for the first time.

THE BILLY "BUCKWHEAT" THOMAS STORY

The timeless shenanigans of the *Our Gang* kids seemed as fresh in the 1950s as they did in the 1930s. When kids from the "baby boomer" generation watched Darla serving lemonade in the summertime, similar stands popped up on neighborhood driveways all across America.

"OTAY!"

After a rapid UN counter-offensive reversing the initial North Korean invasion, the People's Republic of China intervened in support of North Korea. Fighting ended with an armistice that was signed on July 27, 1953.

On May 11, 1956, after one year, eleven months, and twenty-eight days of service, most notably in the 38th Infantry, Light Weapons Infantryman and Private First Class William Thomas transferred from Fort Lewis, Washington to receive an honorable discharge from the Lieutenant H. E. Kroeger and the US Army. He was released from active military service to the Army Reserve to complete eight years' service under Universal Military Training and Service Act. He returned to civilian life proudly decorated with a National Defense Service Medal and a Good Conduct Medal.

Billy was single again, and he had only worked as a child actor, spray painter, and other jobs. The road ahead was one big question mark.

THE BILLY "BUCKWHEAT" THOMAS STORY

May 31, 1962, PFC William Thomas received his Honorable Discharge from Second Lieutenant Garry Standley of the US Army.

"OTAY!"

After leaving the US Army, Billy faced a dilemma shared by many of his co-stars from *Our Gang*. The only work he had ever done was in films. He had to return to civilian life, and he wrestled with the decision of whether to attempt a comeback as an actor or pursue an entirely different line of work. He was offered film and stage roles, but he had no desire to return to Hollywood as an actor.

"I just couldn't see going from studio to studio auditioning, and I knew even the big names had to go through that. It seemed like too much of a rat race," he told writer Richard Lamparski.

Opportunities for actors were difficult to obtain even under the best of circumstances. Black actors faced even tougher challenges, and roles for ex-child stars were rare. He stood at another major crossroad and took careful stock of his options.

THE BILLY "BUCKWHEAT" THOMAS STORY

After Billy left the army, the world would not allow him to grow up. People expected him to eternally be the boy he always was, and he found the going rough to forge a place as a man in the world.

"OTAY!"

In 1953, Billy took stock of his options and thought hard about his work experience. Throughout his years as a child actor, he was exposed to some of the most talented craftsmen at the Hal Roach Studios and at MGM. From them, he had closely observed the various skills and crafts utilized in the making of motion pictures. After considering his choices, he wisely opted to bypass the complicated journey of pursuing an acting career in an industry that he knew offered few opportunities for Black men, and he found work as a Technicolor lab technician at the MGM studios in Culver City, where many of the *Our Gang* shorts were filmed. He ably took his experience in film work and learned the trade of film editing and cutting. Over the following years, he worked on several prominent motion pictures, including Steven Spielberg's *Jaws* (1975) and Michael Anderson's *Logan's Run* (1976).

THE BILLY "BUCKWHEAT" THOMAS STORY

By 1953, Billy was a grown man, but most people only wanted to know him as he was when he was a boy.

"OTAY!"

Throughout the 1950s, Billy's appearances in the *Our Gang* comedies had been resurrected through television, 16mm non-theatrical home-movies, and finally, back to movie theaters. In 1959, Hal Roach brought the proven crowd pleasers back into movie theaters with *Little Rascals Varieties*, a compilation feature-film from Monogram that was made up of five *Our Gang* shorts from the 1930s. The shorts used were *Our Gang Follies of 1936*, *Our Gang Follies of 1938*, *Bored of Education*, *Fishy Tales*, and *Glove Taps*. The cast list read like a Who's Who of the series' alumni with sixty-seven names from Jackie Banning to Joy Wurgaft filling out the roster of names. For audiences that had only experienced the joy of the comedies for the first time on television, seeing them on the big screen as they were meant to be seen in theaters rocking with laughter lit a fuse under the films' never-ending popularity.

THE BILLY "BUCKWHEAT" THOMAS STORY

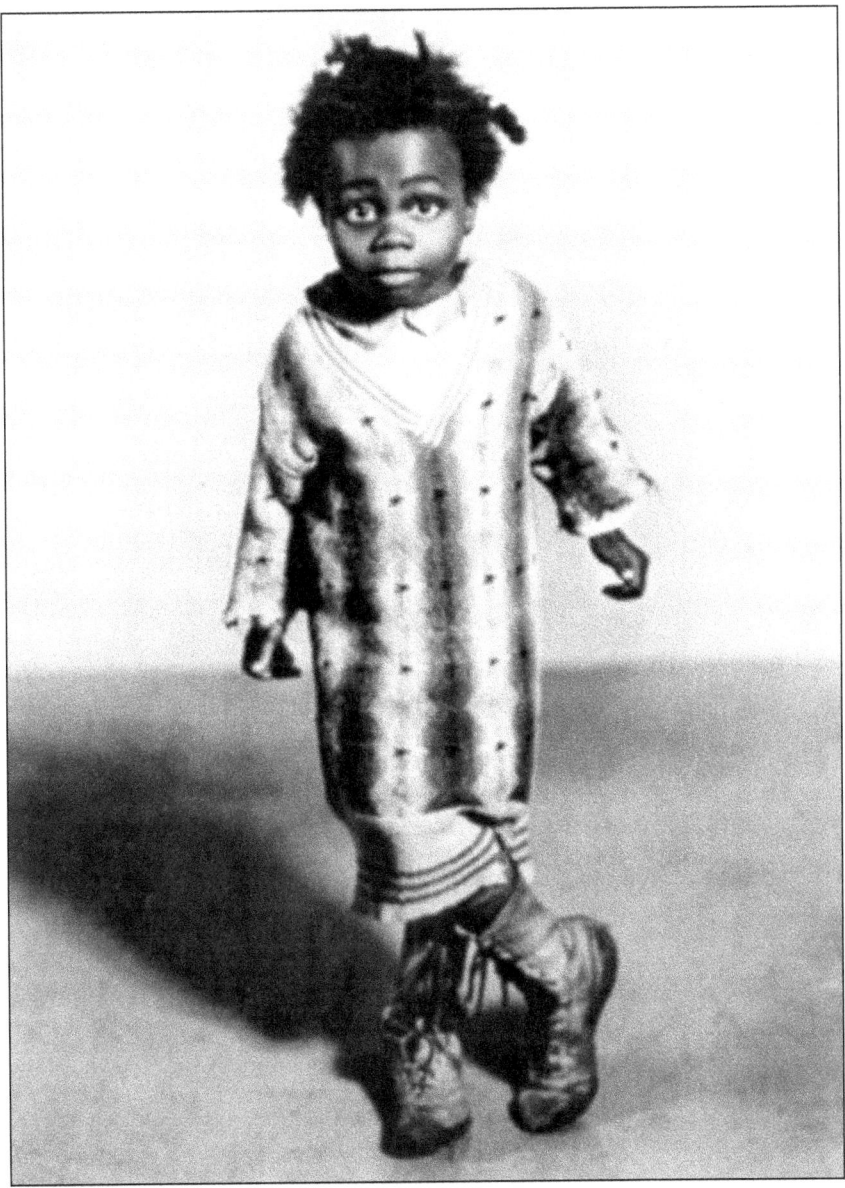

With the Civil Rights movement in full swing, there were those who looked back with disdain on the way Hollywood treated Black American actors in the 1930s, but Billy never thought that he had been forced to embody an insulting image. He often reminded people that all the kids in the *Our Gang* films were lampooned for laughs one way or another.

"OTAY!"

By the 1960s, the Woodstock Music Festival and psychedelic music were factors in a revolution in all areas of the entertainment business. Nostalgia had also become a new American pastime. Broadway audiences were lining up to see Ruby Keeler in *No, No, Nanette*, and Pearl Bailey and Cab Calloway were drawing crowds to see an all-Black production of *Hello Dolly*.

Thanks to the resurgence of interest in *The Little Rascals* on television, people were curious to meet Billy. He was invited to attend premiers, officiate at pageants, and make a comeback, but he stopped short of being too visibly active with those requests. Billy lived a decent, private life with no desire to return to any kind of a heavy schedule that exploited his distant past. He was content to stay home, play his percussion instruments, listen to music, communicate with ham radio operators nationwide, and enjoy his closest friends.

THE BILLY "BUCKWHEAT" THOMAS STORY

Billy in the 1960s (TOP) officiating at a beauty pageant, and (BOTTOM) in his studio/game room at home, where he loved to play percussion instruments.

"OTAY!"

In 1964, Billy visited the Movieland Wax Museum, he was photographed with his cherished *Our Gang* figures. The popular museum featured life-size wax likenesses and was located in Buena Park, California, just one block from Knott's Berry Farm and minutes away from Disneyland. A favorite of tourists year-round, the museum featured over 280 other famous celebrities made out of wax. Original sets with authentic costumes and props completed the masterful illusion.

On the morning of Saturday, March 11, 2006, a once-in-a-lifetime auction took place for the sale of the wax likenesses along with all the props, costumes, furnishings, and ornate chandeliers. Up for auction went the wax figures of Alfalfa, Spanky, Darla, Buckwheat, and Petey, all from the setting of them in *The Awful Tooth*, which starred Billy, Darla Hood, Spanky McFarland, and Carl Switzer. In a flurry of bidding, they all went to a collector for the sum of $5,000.

THE BILLY "BUCKWHEAT" THOMAS STORY

Billy in 1964 at the Movieland Wax Museum in Buena Park, California, in front of the wax figures of Buckwheat and Alfalfa from the setting of them in *The Awful Tooth*.

"OTAY!"

When the old *Our Gang* shorts were circulated anew through television, being the son of "Buckwheat" was not always easy for Bill, Jr.

"Do the kids at school ever tease you about me?" Billy asked his son.

"Almost exactly!" Bill told him, recalling the stories he had heard about the taunting Billy endured in his school years after he left the series.

Bill's newfound notoriety caught Mattie's interest. She developed a deep desire to repeat Billy's childhood film success with her grandson. Bill was only interested in playing sports, and movies would cut in on his time playing baseball. Despite his lack of interest, and without Billy being aware of her plan, Mattie arranged for an audition with producers. Bill was plucked from George Washington Carver Elementary School, dressed in his nicest suit, and carted off to be interviewed at offices where the televisions series *77 Sunset Strip* was filmed.

THE BILLY "BUCKWHEAT" THOMAS STORY

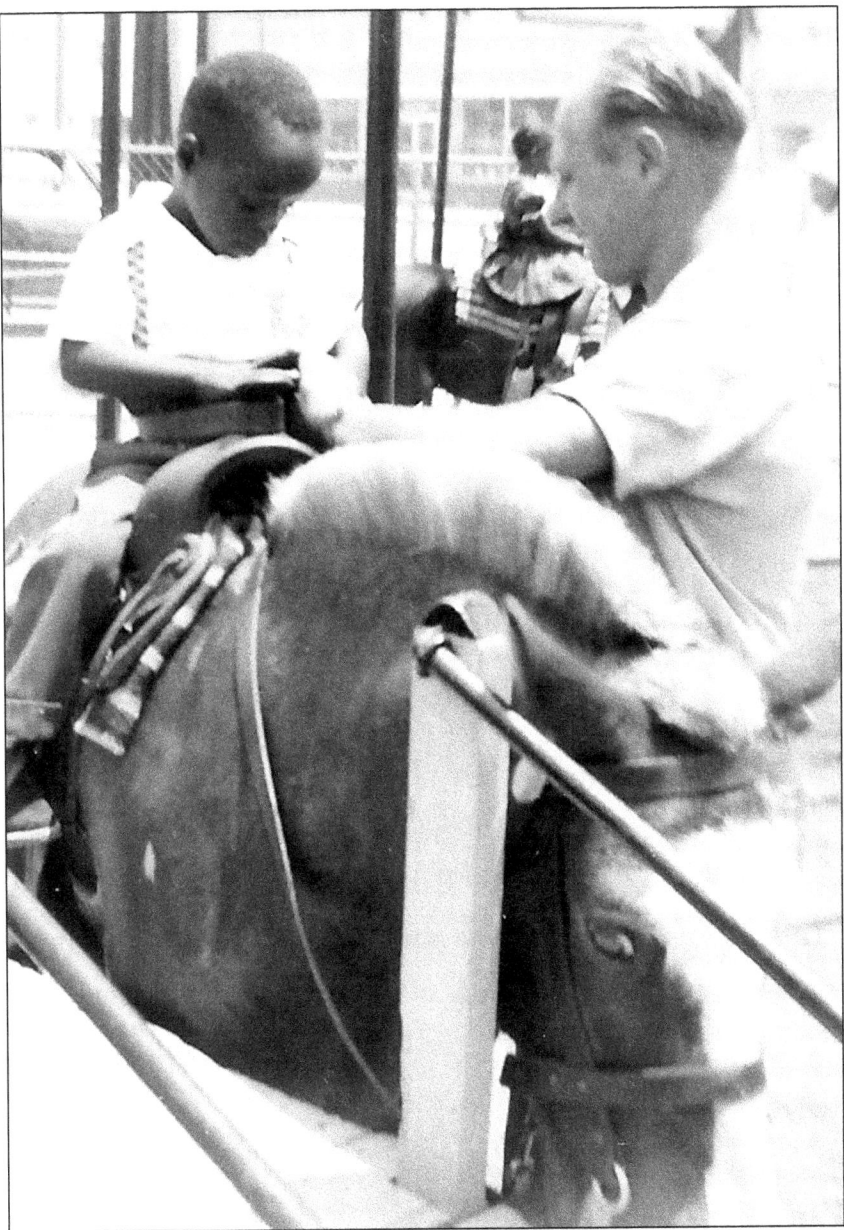

Mattie watched Bill, Jr. closely as he grew. She was filled with a growing certainty that lightning would strike twice if only she could get him into the movies, so she waited only a few more years before enacting her plan to make him become "Buckwheat II."

"OTAY!"

Lillie, Bill's other grandmother, led him up a long, winding stairs to film producer's offices.

"I don't want to do it!" Bill protested repeatedly.

At first, producers found Bill difficult to interview. He was shy around the gruff businessmen, and they had to walk him outside to get him to relax, but their efforts were to no avail. They paired him with a blonde, female staff member, and only then did he loosen up enough to momentarily forget sports and talk about being in a film, but she got the same kind response from him.

"I don't want to be in the movies," Bill kept saying.

Despite his protests, Bill was made to pose for a studio portrait next to a stool. The overactive youth hated the whole experience. At each of the interviews, he steadfastly told the producers that he did not want to be in the movies.

THE BILLY "BUCKWHEAT" THOMAS STORY

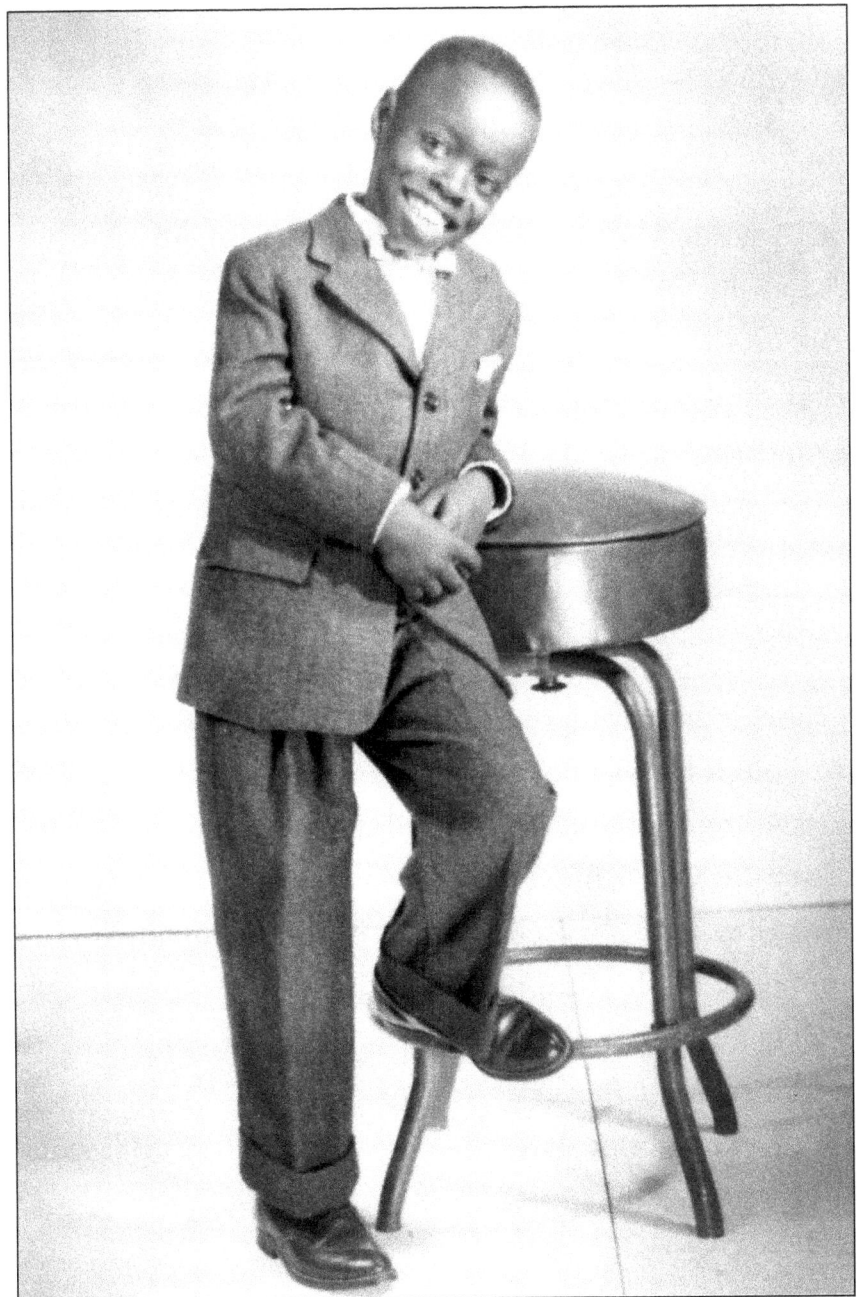

Bill Jr. was asked to pose for a studio portrait while his grandmother tried in vain to get him enthusiastic about being an actor in the movies. All he wanted to do was play baseball.

"OTAY!"

Casting the son of "Buckwheat" in their new film kept producers interested. Lillie duly shepherded Bill up the horribly long, winding staircase, full of hope that Hollywood lightning would strike twice with her grandson.

A second interview led to a third, but Bill was missing school and baseball to return for callbacks. Finally, he hit upon a desperate measure. He deliberately tripped and fell on the long winding staircase. Lillie grabbed him, but the fall seemed to have hurt him. Although he was not seriously injured, producers were forced to face the fact that he did not want to cooperate. They allowed Lillie to take him away for the last time and they sadly watched their hope for an intriguing publicity angle disappear with him.

"He doesn't want to do it!" Mattie finally had to admit to Bill's mother.

"It was never in my blood to be an actor," Bill said.

THE BILLY "BUCKWHEAT" THOMAS STORY

Bill, Jr. grew up a fine young seventeen-year-old, the captain of the baseball team and on the football team in 1968 at Verbun Dei High School.

"OTAY!"

Darla Hood organized an *Our Gang/Little Rascals* reunion to be sponsored by the Los Angeles Chapter of The Sons of the Desert, but she died on June 13, 1979. True to their promises, everyone rallied together in August 1980. The gathering was Billy's last meeting with his old chums. In the famous reunion photo, those attending included (standing in back row) Billy, Edith Fellows, Eugene "Pineapple" Jackson, Marvin "Bubbles" Strin, Sidney "The Woim" Kibrick, Joe Cobb, Sons of the Desert member Grand Sheik Bob Satterfield, Ernie "Sunshine Sammy" Morrison, Leonard Landy, George "Spanky" McFarland, Tommy "Butch" Bond, Delmar Watson, and Butch Bond, Jr. Those seated in front included Dorothy "Echo" DeBorba, Verna Kornman, mother of Mildred and Mary Kornman, Peggy Ahearn, Mildred Kornman, and Sons of the Desert organizer Earl Kress. Those kneeling in front were Sons of the Desert members Armand Lewis and author Richard Bann.

THE BILLY "BUCKWHEAT" THOMAS STORY

(TOP) In 1980, *Our Gang* stars Joe Cobb, Spanky McFarland, and Buckwheat Thomas reunited at (BOTTOM) Billy's last *Our Gang* meeting—Los Angeles, August 1980.

"OTAY!"

Billy told Richard Lamparski, "I've got a good-looking son who's never given me one minute of trouble. I've got kids knocking on my door all the time, and I happen to love kids. I've got good friends, a nice house, and I drive a Cadillac. I think I've been a lucky person."

Billy became somewhat reclusive. He avoided attending Darla Hood's funeral by saying he was out of town. He worked at Deluxe General, but after work, he retired to his home and played with his ham radio and electronics. He seldom went out, and his friends began to notice. Even Stymie Beard was worried. He told Bill to spend more time with his father. Bill called him and asked if anything was wrong. Billy said, "No, I just think I need to go on a diet. If I don't lose some weight, I'll be dead before I turn fifty."

THE BILLY "BUCKWHEAT" THOMAS STORY

Billy in 1980 just a few weeks before his death enjoying the sight of his work in the window of a Los Angeles shop.

"OTAY!"

In early October 1980, Billy's neighbors realized that they had not seen him for several days and they were concerned enough to call police. At approximately 4:30 p.m., Officer Philip Spada investigated the call and visited Billy's southwest Los Angeles home. After no reply came to his repeated knocks at the front door, Spada opened a window and climbed inside. He found Billy dead. Later, his death was determined to have been on October 10 from a sudden heart attack. Ironically, he died exactly forty-six years to the day he was signed as a little rascal. He was forty-nine years old.

On Monday, October 20, 1980, services were held at Angelus Crenshaw Chapel, with Father Hanley officiating. Active pallbearers included Lewis Long, Manuel Garcia, Melvin Rischer, Leo Dukes, Lewis Carriere, and Fletcher Theus. In a touching opening, services began with the "Theme from the Little Rascals."

THE BILLY "BUCKWHEAT" THOMAS STORY

(TOP) Billy's funeral service memorial card. (BOTTOM) Billy's gravestone in Inglewood Park Cemetery, Los Angeles, California.

"OTAY!"

THE BILLY "BUCKWHEAT" THOMAS STORY

"OTAY!"

THE BILLY "BUCKWHEAT" THOMAS STORY

"OTAY!"

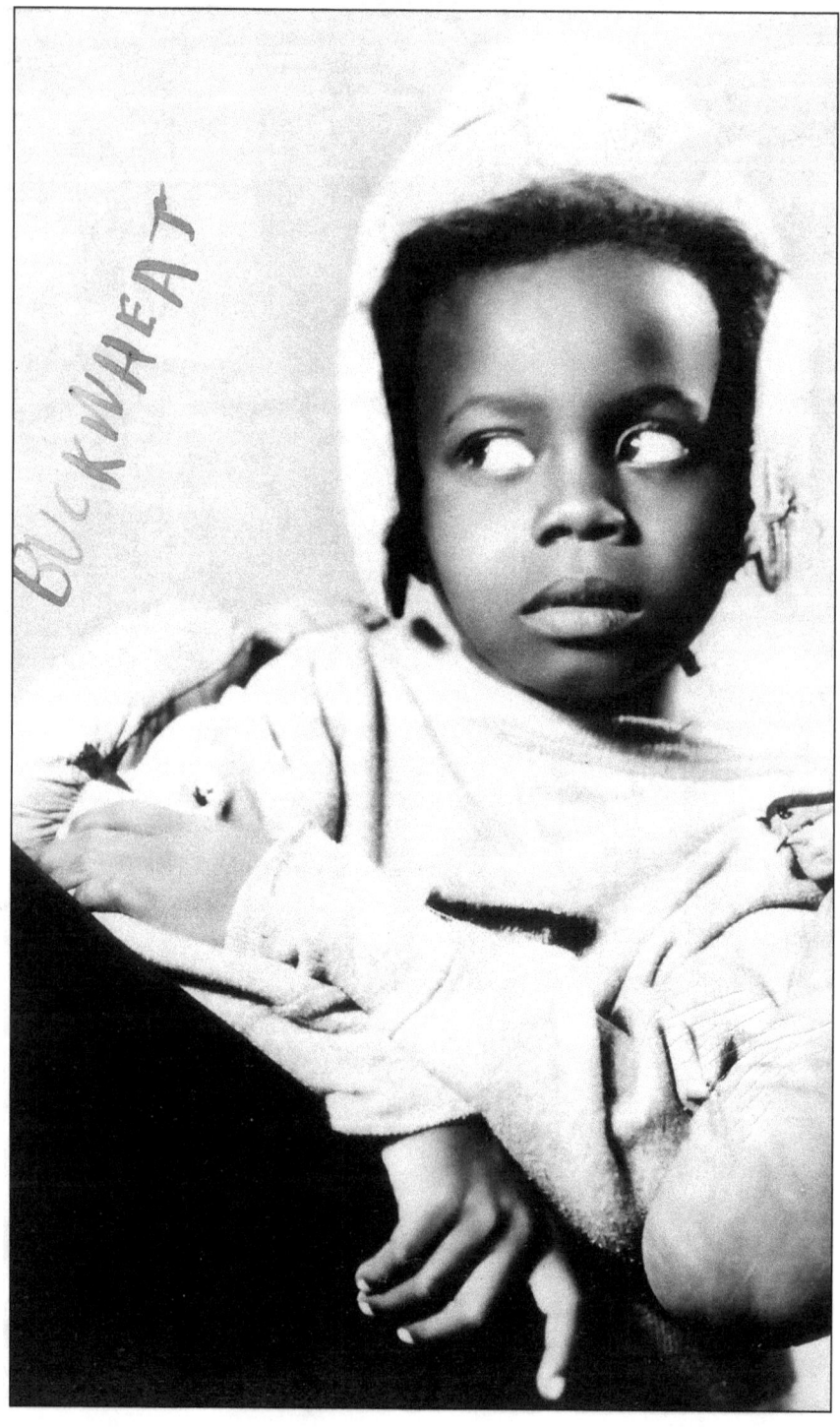

THE BILLY "BUCKWHEAT" THOMAS STORY

Bibliography

"A Buckwheat Wannabe Lands 20/20 on the Griddle." *People Magazine*, October 20, 1990.

"Buckwheat: Preserving Actor's Legacy." The *Los Angeles Times*, November 8, 1992.

"Children are Charming, But Jokes are Bad in Rascals." The *Syracuse Herald Journal*, August 5, 1994, page 104.

Cooper, Jackie. *Please Don't Shoot My Dog*. New York: William Morrow and Company, Inc. 1981.

"Ebonics According to Buckwheat, a New Furor over Black English Provokes Some Stereotypical Thinking." By Jack E. White in *Time*, January 13, 1997.

"Great Colored Find." The *La Crosse Tribune and Leader-Press*, February 28, 1937, page 9.

"Hal Roach — Last Link to a Glorious Entertainment Era." By Charles Chaplin in The *Los Angeles Times*, November 4, 1992.

Hess, Gary R. *Presidential Decisions for War: Korea, Vietnam and the Persian Gulf*. New York: Johns Hopkins University Press, 2001.

"He Wasn't Buckwheat, 20-20 Acknowledges. The *Los Angeles Times*, October 9, 1990.

"Idea Man Wins Payoff At Last." The *Chester Times*, September 23, 1955, page 20.

THE BILLY "BUCKWHEAT" THOMAS STORY

Lloyd, Harold. *An American Comedy*. New York: Stein Dover Publications, 1971.

Maltin, Leonard and Richard Bann. *Our Gang: The Life and Times of the Little Rascals*. New York: Crown Publishers, 1977.

"Personal Appearances." By Louella O. Parsons in the *Waterloo Daily Courier*, April 15, 1936, page 15.

Schickel, Richard. *Harold Lloyd: The Shape of Laughter*. New York: New York Graphic Society, 1974.

"Sean Young Nets 2 Glden Raspberries" by W. Speers in the *Philadelphia Inquirer*, March 31, 1992.

Shales, Tom W. and James Andrew Miller. *Live From New York: an Uncensored History of Saturday Night Live*. Boston: Back Bay Books, 2003.

Steen, Mike. *Hollywood Speaks! An Oral History*. New York: G. P. Putnam's Sons. 1974.

"The Little Rascals Film Review." By Janet Maslin in the *New York Times*, August 5, 1994.

"The Son of William Thomas." By Richard Johnson in the *Daily News*, March 30, 1992.

"Hollywood '80 The Second International Convention of Sons of the Desert." By Tim Doherty in *Pratfall*, 1982.

Ward, Richard Lewis. *A History of the Hal Roach Studios*. Carbondale: Southern Illinois University Press. 2005.

"Who Played Buckwheat Role is Now Bone of Contention." The *Danville Register*, December 8, 1976, page 24.

www.ingramcontent.com/pod-product-compliance
Lightning Source LLC
Chambersburg PA
CBHW071458160426
43195CB00013B/2154